Rock and Lodestone

Rock and Lodestone

Glenda Kerney Brown

For Mum,
whose imprint lives on every page,
in me, and in all I could ever wish to be,
love never fades.

For Tim, my soulmate and hero,
who gifts me strength, laughter
and limitless support.

And for Deb,
who believed in me.

To all of them, I shall be eternally grateful.

A good book is a blessing

Copyright ©2016 Bennison Books
Copyright Glenda Kerney Brown
All rights reserved
First published 2016

This book is sold subject to the condition that it shall not be reproduced in any form without the prior written permission of the author and Bennison Books. Brief quotations may be used without permission in articles or reviews.

Bennison Books Poetic Licence

A good book is a blessing

Contents

Introduction 1
About the Author 3
The Box 7
Part One: Shark 9
   Optic Neuritis 1: Sea Change on Baildon Bank 1993 11
   Optic Neuritis 2: Remission 1993 13
   The Rainbow 14
   Caught 15
   Things I'd Love to Tell Her 16
   The Wrecking Crew 17
   Strong 1994 18
   Some Days 19
   Shadow 1994 20
   Glory 21
   Strange Self 1994 22
   Memo to Self 23
   Breathing 24
   Melancholy 25
   Holidaymakers 26
   Collected Six Times a Year from Respite 27
   Persephone 29
   Relapse and Respond 1996 32
Part Two: Rock and Lodestone 33
   Change Before and Beyond 35
   Hands and Wheels 36

- Cloud Formation 37
- On Waking 38
- Sonnet for Us 39
- One Choice 40
- Love's Market 41
- Explorer 43
- Memory Relaxes 44
- Life Before This 45

Part Three: Slivers of Light 47

- Strange Horse 49
- Pit Pony 50
- Rough Horses 51
- Songs of Making 52
- Animal Eden 1920 53
- Descendants 54
- The First Cat is Reflected 55
- Cat Couture: Instructions for Wearing 56
- Conversations with my Cats: 1 Victory at Axminster 58
- Conversations with my Cats: 2 Long Gone Beloveds 59
- Goodnight My Darling Girl 60
- Dorcas from Time to Time 61
- Three Minutes of Butterfly Now 62
- Kestrel 63
- Sharks 64
- The Flatey Experience 65
- The Lurcher 67

Part Four: Across Time 69

- Sorrow 71
- Across Time and Space 72
- Pre-mourning 73

The Singing Sea 74
Do Not Ignore Now's Moment Come What
May 75
Layers 76
Icelandic Lady 77
Ancestors 79
I Carry Her With Me 80
Fossil Speak 81
The Silver Door 82
The Necessity of Play 83
Modern-Day Miracles 84
A Story of Air 85
The Road 86
The Oak 90
Rage 91
Green Lane 92
The Need for Protection 93
Good Hearts 95
Three Days of Christmas 96
The Case 97

Part Five: Green Daze 99

The Glen Woods 101
Green Daze 103
Garden Grass 104
One Chevin December 105
Shell Dreaming 106
Winter Prison 108
Bad Spring 109
'77 Hot Summer Drops 111
The Crying Leaves 112
September View 113
Goit Stock 114

Part Six: Epiphany 115
    Leaving...117
    From the Other Side..118
    Old Man Gone..119
    Faces..120
    Laments...122
    The Mirror..124
    Insha Allah 2015...125
    Play Day Diaries 126
    On a Southport Sunday.......................................127
    Dvořák in Bradford..130

Introduction

With these endlessly inventive and marvellous poems Glenda Kerney Brown explores the things that she values, the things that she cleaves to, and the underlying tragedy of our human experience, which is that we inevitably lose (or are lost to) the things we love. Art has the power to hold back and make sense of this tide of loss, and with an artist's palette Glenda commemorates the past, celebrates the present and contemplates the future in honest and beautiful poetry.

None of these poems are long (I would argue that they are all of exactly the right length) but they each contain a world of imagery, wisdom and experience out of proportion to their size on the page. Glenda looks at her family, her animals, landscape and nature, and, in language that is suffused with a vibrant intelligence, illuminates them all to us.

The title 'Rock and Lodestone' has a medieval flavour to it, from a time before compasses, when travellers relied on more primitive ways of finding their way around a largely unknown world; and, of course, many of the poems in this very fine, first collection deal with Glenda's journey into MS, its mysterious and uncharted waters, and the challenges and limitations found there. But the poems are about the triumph of the human spirit, of snatching victory from what seems to be unavoidable extinction, and allowing the reader the privilege of experiencing some of that journey too.

Let me suggest that you savour the poems in this collection and you will meet and begin to get to know the extraordinary poet and human being that is Glenda Kerney Brown.

James Nash 2016

James Nash is a British poet. His work, published by Valley Press, includes Some Things Matter: 63 Sonnets, *described as 'magical and memorable' by Sarah Waters (Booker-shortlisted novelist); 'wonderful' and 'assured' by Ian Duhig (three times T.S. Eliot Prize shortlisted poet); and 'a thing of beauty' by Justin Cartwright (Booker-shortlisted novelist).* www.jamesnash.co.uk

About the Author

I stumbled into poetry, mainly because I could no longer pursue the one thing I knew I was any good at, which was acting – actors usually have all their limbs present and correct. Thanks to multiple sclerosis I can claim only the first half of that statement for all of mine. My eyes are wonky as well, with no possibility of unwonking them. Why am I not on the scrapheap? Just lucky, I guess. Then, of course, there's all of the following.

I grew up in a small village in West Yorkshire, called Baildon, where moorland, heathland, woodland, rivers and a canal were within easy reach. I had a mum who took me to all of these, and who later, with good fortune and hard graft, provided two ponies in succession so that I could explore them for myself. This was my grounding in nature which has become the fertile soil for much of my poetry. Also, my love of horses, which has never left me. I yearn for them still, but at least I am one of the lucky ones who have known them at all.

The other love that I was gifted as a child was animals. We always had two cats of different ages, so that as one left us, after a time, we could have a kitten from the local milkman's farm. These were wonderful days, ripe for poetry. Then our dogs found us and decided to stay. Oh, lucky us.

Mum had read books to me ad infinitum as I was growing up, and introduced me to the world of drama which I went on to study at Swansea University, along with English.

I didn't return to Baildon to live for many years, during which time I got my diagnosis of MS. I went nearly blind in one eye, but then sight came back (nearly), whereupon the other eye followed suit, but that also came back (nearly). I had to have some way of coming to grips with it all, and that way was poetry. After that, I had another eight years of doing what I wanted, when I wanted, and enjoying myself thoroughly, almost as if the diagnosis had never happened.

Of course, it has found me again and I'm now in a wheelchair, with both arms and hands very shaky. I write using a voice interactive program for which I'm incredibly grateful, and I listen endlessly to books, including poetry, of course.

I know this all sounds very grim, but it's not. I adapted. I can't act any more, but I rediscovered that I love writing poetry. I wrote poems for children about a 'dogmother' which I have performed at primary schools but, oh, joy, I joined a local writing class, run by the incomparable James Nash, and began to write poetry full-time for adults which I have now done for over two years.

Writing poetry has now become what I am: I can lose myself in it for hours, to re-emerge physically tired but mentally invigorated. What more could I ask?

I have a wondrous husband who is also my full-time carer. I already had MS when we met, and he has had the courage and fortitude to travel this journey with me. He enables me to do what I do best and I love him to bits.

Of course, there were the bad days when I 'graduated' from limping, to using a stick, two sticks, a walker, and eventually a wheelchair, all within a couple of years. But I have now been stable for over four years, and although I know this won't last forever, for now, it's more than enough.

All proceeds from this book will be donated to the Multiple Sclerosis Trust.

The Box

The box is black, olden, Eastern,
bearing swaddled symbols,
embers of fire in the memory:
kin koi carp in mid-leap, lunging,
lilies leaning, pinned with butterflies,
and butterflies, butterflies, lifting
the mottled green leaves, which trail
direct from the islands of Japan.

Kin is a Japanese word pertaining specifically to koi carp, meaning golden metallic.

Part One
Shark

Optic Neuritis 1: Sea Change on Baildon Bank 1993

I wade on footpaths I have run
before my sea-change;
now damage has become my home.

Birds cartwheel fragmented fins
to crash in static corals where
once beeches played in sunshine;
far below the muted purrs
of deadly barracudas winding
single-minded ways along the road
do not disturb my change.

Vast estates of broken roofs
revert to a bed of ancient slate
on which I may soon lie,
or glide above, in hunger,
knowing nothing but my purpose.

The lichened lids I cannot shut have crusted,
damned my younger sight,
when this was more well-known than dolls
and boys whose heads were cradled

in its heather.

I find refuge in millstone grit
and 'ware the hounds –
I cannot have their certain
friendliness dismayed and melted
to confusion as they sense
a damaged work and let me be –
they rough and tumble past,
too fast for my fish eyes.

I suck in tide and slide
dissolving fingertips on
skull, brow and jaw,
oily nape and shoulder down
the breastbone to the ribs,
hunting for my gills;

they must form,
they must;
how else can I breathe?

under the oceans of my sight I must translate,
or else I shall couch here
until my bones are bracken-bleached
and fish eyes lie like marbles
in the heather.

Optic Neuritis 2: Remission 1993

I am not fish
I am not fish
I am the tender grass
of springtime scorched
and dreaming I will
never drown again;

these eyes now merely flinch
before the day's glaring uncertainty
but if I dare to wither under this,
dear God, do not bring back old oceans,
send instead a season's gentle rain
to ease the life out of the dust,
and numb the pain.

These two poems burst out as I was trying to come to terms with my sight failing. All I had was a diagnosis of optic neuritis, there was no mention of MS until after the second eye's relapse when I was told, by mistake, through the post. Baildon is the village I grew up in and the Bank a wonderful heathland where I would walk the dogs.

The Rainbow

There is a rainbow we can walk under,
over and through, drenching ourselves in health,
but you will lie, plank flat, as the chosen pass by.

Only twice have you wept your shuddering skin
    off,
through all these granite years, when you could not
    find
another boulder to add to your mountain of try.

Caught

One hundred thousand trapped
in a net, hooked
on any whiff of possibility of cure.
Isolated, gasping for normality,
somehow swimming strongly, mostly.

Things I'd Love to Tell Her

On the day the towers fell, her legs began to crumble,
sure foundations faultered and sweet life began its
    tumble
into the deep.

Sly fate would not give notice of its sure horizons
    then,
but may suffuse her drowning with exquisite oxygen
from depths unknown.

Lady, presumption of grief to come is a stagnant cell:
cloaked years may yet bejewel you with showers of
    such miracles
they staunch all tears.

The Wrecking Crew

You wrote there is an iceberg, upon which
we'll wreck ourselves; it looms in the dark,
a titanic shark; pale, undetectable
until it strikes, and all hands and legs are lost.

Strong 1994

What is Strong?
How do you know you've got enough?
How do you square up to fate?
Or use your Strong to fight it?

To fight fate? Not even that,
not worth fate yet,
just one of its quirks.

Jesus Christ! Beat hell out of a quirk?
With what? Can I grab it by the throat
and slam it up against a wall,
fist in its face and screaming?

I know what it would do.
The lousy quirk would whine,
"I'll set my DAD on you,"
and howl with laughter
as I pass out cold.

Bastard.

Some Days

Some days the sun reaches inside my heart,
raises it up to a halcyon place,
mellowness drifting through bone, far apart
from sorrow I know I cannot erase;
dead-eyed it squats, silhouetting sharp shreds
of helplessness, keening, tempting despair,
wrapped in a frisson of dread that's unsaid,
under the sun, I know fair is not fair.
The warrior fights her self-proclaimed foe,
exploits known weaknesses, wages campaigns,
I fight a war, whether I will or no,
myself, the enemy, parley disdains;
I champion strength, true love wipes my brow,
but some days the bastard wins anyhow.

Shadow 1994

There is a darkening shadow at my heels,
pale weight, formless; where it lies, it crushes.
My mother hurls herself into its path –
selfless love and useless reason,
my brother tries to solve it in the dark
and my friends mouth prayers from a distant place:
the shadow falls, relentless, voiding all,
cast by a helpless one, powerless, numb.

Glory

Shit happens. Relentlessly we clamber
inside ourselves to examine the damage
for an hour, a week, a minute, a lifetime,
chew each acrid morsel in hope of
deciphering the passion and the glory.

Gaily I wade through brown and solitary life,
ignoring the clangs of my distress,
standing on tiptoe for a whiff of heaven.

Strange Self 1994

Ah, strange self, it's you.
Once again, before your face
I dissolve in a moment only,
flesh under acid; before you,
the colours of the world dissolve
and in your recognition,
ah ... the moment of despair.

Memo to Self

Light one last candle for me,
while I wait for the stars to arrive,
stars that will call my name,
heal my grief, and take me inside joy.

Tonight the world is heavy,
and a little too long, so curl up my legs
on the sofa, and gently move the cat,
don't think about tomorrow,
only light me one last candle
and place it in the window
while I wait for the stars to arrive.

Breathing

Your toes squeeze ocean bedded, alien sands.
Let go, breathe now, feed loaves to multicoloured fishes!
Inside the goldfish bowl on your head, follow your own
glossy bubbles racing to the sun; remember this;

three-tone grey shapes jerk your head down,
stream steadily under a mask too small to hold;
attached to life through a tube, you strain to follow;
Spinners spin your life on silent threads; remember this;

an angel zooms up close, pauses the world, black wings
the speed of light; delivers a lengthy sermon on guzzling
nectar from the source; drink this and remember;

below a branch of concrete safety, his measured blink
acknowledges; speechless, you have spoken with a God;
he pads on in striped and rhythmic glory; you leave God
to his cage, rattle off in yours.

At night and in the day, your dead legs on the bed,
the spectre of things breaking down keeps vigil.
Retrieve the miracles of fish, dolphin, hummingbird
and tiger. Retrieve your life, your breath!

Melancholy

Today, melancholy has drifted in and clouded me,
things are become unsaid; something has broken,
does anybody know what it is? I slope around,
can't plump up the will to do, vague efforts
diminish me. This room is unspeakably warm;
my blue vase holds blotches of spindly flowers,
which I may rearrange, or not;
Matisse should paint me now as I drain,
ring my staring eyes in kohl, or I may become a cat,
forever glassy eyed, watching the hours fade away.

Holidaymakers

Plonked down beside the unnaturally
blue lake, a muscular building inhales
a new batch, coughs, exhales the old.

Bubbly volunteers froth up to aid
full-time carers with postcode conditions,
MS, CP, CF, strokes, and obscurer;

they party down, drunk on freedom,
out for a week, or two, or even three,
on ale, wine, digits of neat whiskey;

she stares out of a streaky window,
streaky eyed, thinks of Switzerland,
pale, blank, vast; perhaps next year.

Collected Six Times a Year from Respite

You would scramble, leggily, into the car, if you could,
are instead a weighty package.
He is all dark cloud and megalith, straps you down in
    grunts.

Once a-dreary-gain, you nibble grey miles,
slide past opaque futures in suburban slop;
attempts at conversation leak clichés.

Traffic light limbos rack up purgatorial minutes,
repetitious impediments, until limp
sunshine faints on utopia's slip road.

The engine simpers, vibrating sweet spots …
The monolith lives! Bounces, three times, pure boy,
summons never-never land in a cherub's grin
that is free, plush and yours with
three lane heaven and molasses!

You rip up humdrums, bastards, chaff;
Your Pan delivers a shocking coup de grâce,
"My name's Peter – and I go like Fuck!"
The car splinters to chrome-plated giggles

which ricochet cock-a-doodle-doos.

Respite is a break for full-time carers, as much as a 'holiday' for the disabled.

Persephone

The lady in the wheelchair walks in her dreams,
    wonderless,
mercifully ignorant of the impossible;
caught in a kaleidoscope of now,
sifting shiny pearls from the past,
oblivious of the disaster of waking
which will punch her in the gut and in the head.
The blows jab up the daily shock of Hades, reigniting
    the pain
of a despairing diagnosis tumbling over itself to greet
    her.

She must toil to put out the strife, persuade her paper
    life to unfold,
feign to be herself; so amazingly brave, so cheerful, so
    in and not in demand,
so brave; so canned for consumption.

Drugs deconstruct her defences, self-pity ebbs and
    flows,
she clutches at myriad younger selves,
flails them into the slippery present, fails to prevent
    their pale, fractured faces
sinking back into the silt of lost opportunities.

In the vast, winter dark her terrified body
    malfunctions;
collapses, flat as cardboard, awaiting collection
by the peace of paramedics.

Time tenderly safeguards her seconds,
knits them into manageable minutes,
realigns twisted hours, combing out the tears;
restores her fragile frame, to dream again.

Bullies are buck-naked, stacked, barbecued,
they taste of stupidity, power and belligerence,
a four course, fat splattering, red blood, molar driven
    chomp;
fishy gossips gape, tongues tied, flapping silently,
icy eyes black, thoughtless and crunchy;
they quiver and slither deliciously down the
    oesophagus;
all are sacrificed endlessly upon her avaricious altar:
the air smells of vengeance and sulphur.

Zeus's panzer divisions rumble off into the wings,
cotton wool balls bump in a cerulean sky,
Aurora entices with technicolour titbits,
a sullen, juvenile sun matures as Apollo chases his sister
around the old oak tree and at the last,
Persephone, Wheelchair Lady, comes out to play.

She wakes, renewed, forgiving and forgiven,
triceps and biceps flex, firing like pistons;
she is gaiety and titanium, her spokes forged in
    Hephaestus' fire,
her revelation, spring and wonderment;
tributes are trilled; daffodils trumpet her triumphant
    regeneration,
tulips turn their heads at her passing, bees perform
bespoke, if bumbling, flypasts:
her old pal Time is reborn and, like a puppy, jumps
    up to greet her:
she has become herself.

Relapse and Respond 1996

I dreamed that yesterday a lump of flesh was
 skewered here,
pierced by the gaze of dead ones drifting slowly down
 to silt;

I dreamed that yesterday my love was passion flayed
 by rage,
which left its baby skin for wolves of grief as black as
 night;

I dreamed in hollow dread of tempests raging all within
a single tear, which burst and drowned a flight of
 angels pure;

today I woke to clarity, to think and know and feel –
sensation sweet and holy nestles safely in my soul.

Part Two
Rock and Lodestone

Change Before and Beyond

Continents cuddle, and promenade their drowning dance,
create countries with each gasp for breath. I breathe you
    in,
evolve my world around your pulsing form, and your
    long,
white arms make my unlooked for Southern Cross.

Dusk stretched clouds finger the world, pull back, push
    out, pull back,
push out, and the endless, crying night reaches
    somewhere, for someone.
I watch your sleeping lashes, pale upon pale; I cannot
    quiet
your jerking dreams, nor rouse your imperfections; still I
    try.

Change, dilated, drags us into being, spring out of
    autumn,
after winter, flicks us to the dark. Or is it light upon light,
floating us above, or in, or through the sun, atoms alive
inside that thing called love, understanding that thing is all
    there is.

Hands and Wheels

Hands, pale and slender,
are you praying to the white moon?
Fluttering,
hiding in the wrinkles of time?
Is your dance begun,
whirling about your silver wheels,
spinning in star-drenched abandon?
Do you speak for lips,
moistened, silent, breathless, waiting?
Does he caress you,
his fingers light as papyrus,
feathers in the winds of desire?
Are you holding him,
in your element, Eden bound?

Cloud Formation

They form slowly, the clouds, indecisive,
vaguely nagging mist on autumn's tongue;
we brown, drink August in September,
the roses, petals packed, confused as we.

Your face is dipped in concentration,
limed by work, the pro bono saviour;
I try not to watch, you don't like that;
cobblestone clouds appear, resolute;
the cat rushes off, we batten down.

Metal wheels weld us close and apart;
Star-crossed years accumulate in silence;
we bob, divided by and on an ocean,
groping for life rafts of coping.

On Waking

Half asleep, you smile the sweetest smile the world has known,
sweeter than the first strawberry, the first tottering lamb,
gangling fawn, whiff of sweetest peas, lark famously ascending
or Romeo as he moves rhythmically upon Juliet, knowing

love at first sight exists. Each morning, knowing the same,
I turn my head, see your dear face upon my pillow, wait;
there it is, as your eyes open on mine. Then you remember.

Sonnet for Us

When thoughtlessly I turn to meet your eyes,
the ripest recognition floods me through,
in blind and helpless love, my old world dies,
calling to question things I thought I knew.
The new life sucks us in, we have no choice,
no chance to mull "Could this be my true love?
How do we differ? Will it be their voice
I'll tune to all my life, or get sick of?"
Cold time is dealing out relentless hands,
would we have looked away, if we but knew?
You cry "No! we must live by fate's commands,
Hold tight our nightly vows of 'I love you'."
So now we battle on, and as I dim,
You care for me, and though I sink, we swim.

One Choice

Two roads may well diverge within a wood;
maiden, with star-crossed love your heart did ache,
in complicated turmoil, poised, you stood –
then chose your mother's love to not forsake.
Was it the tougher of the roads? Of course,
you severed two ripe hearts with one blind blow,
you sent his heart away, cut off its source,
your heart, source-less, stricken, to hell must go;
his living words, uttered one winter's night,
wrapped in your wiser lips, the cracks prevail,
bleeding his letters, he whose heart's delight
in life and loving you, would never fail:
God, rewind time! I'd thrust you if I could,
onto that other road less understood.

Love's Market

"My love, leave the market!" he dropped to one knee,
pulsating with ardour and but one Chablis,
"The fairest of flowers, Lady, you are she.
You must not be married, unless it's to me.
Love's market is tawdry, a scramble at best,
pray leave it behind; Heaven, grant my request!
Your head on my heart in our nuptial nest."
She gazed down upon him, had she heard his cry?
The Seraphim scrambled to hear her reply.
"My dear," she sighed softly, "you mustn't despair,
but I love this market; I breathe it as air,
it's vital, it's vibrant, it sizzles, scot-free
of life's little boredoms, how lucky are we,
we children of Cupid? Sweet man, you must see
you're the third one this week to ask for my hand,
it's wondrous that I am so much in demand.
Of course, there's my fortune; ridiculous thing
which I feign to squander, without any ring,
I never would, never could give you the trouble
Of trying to spend it; your pulse rate would double!
No dear, I must selflessly now put you first,
or your heart would certainly suffer the worst.
I glimpse twinges now as you rise from one knee –
take heart, like your rivals, you're younger than me,

a mere eighty-two to my eighty-three, BUT
statistics suggest that you'll not outlast me.
I must then endure my fortune and lark it,
drowning me in the champagne of love's market!"
Great cheers floated down from the heavens above
as angels yelled "HOUSE!" on the call of "True Love!"

Explorer

Was I once a traveller, an explorer, a greyhound
chasing horizons, swiping our complacent God's delicates,
casting my fate into the world's ocean, risking it all for you?
Did I stagger to your door, fainting under the weight
of gold, ivory, hallowed perfumes of Arabi and more?
Perhaps my simple heart thirsted to bring you Asia's
    full-bodied
chrysanthemums, tendrilled ferns, date-laden palms
and the love-leaved cyclamen of the Mediterranean?
Or did I perish in a crowded dhow off Zanzibar,
your salty name on my lips, returned to the ocean of souls
which jostle for birth? I will not jostle, I will wait for you:
slivers of life entwined, we shall leap again, together.

Memory Relaxes

Before cold curses fur our tongues,
strive to crack the rock and lodestone,
we retrieve the old Mauritian paradise:
supine, under its southern cross, I chart the
slow-burning comet of your smile.

Before the rock is hammered, the lodestone
twisted or warped, we retrieve the simple thrust
of Pitlochry, twinned with salmon in the dark,
beg the juices of the world that bit us,
"Climax in our veins and flood us out!"

Breathing slows, wire untwists; the cornerstone
is sure, the lodestone's flame true North.
As relief pads round an un-shocked room,
    we breakfast.

Life Before This

I'll tell you about life before this,
remember it? We had one,
before the painful state of now,
before the world shrank to a teacup.

Before the slopping and the shouting,
before the chair, before the hoist,
before the endless state of care,
winter cracking in your voice.

I tell of giggles you unleashed,
joyful puppies racing the sun,
the astonishment of existence
hard at their heels, trumpeting.

I tell of a buttered tummy, rolling
past parasols to land on your smile;
moon mugged on African sands,
the world bites into us, whole.

I blaze the neediness of independence,
shriek erratically against the hard way,
find that every crevice of every road,
returns to you, my rock and lodestone.

Part Three
Slivers of Light

Strange Horse

It is the strangest horse I ride through glades of
　　darkest hue,
some animals come not near us, perhaps some
　　others do;
its colour I cannot decide, it ebbs and flows with
　　time,
it breathes the laughter in my days as dying
　　bluebells chime.
The sharpest rocks it leaps straight o'er,
as if they have no place by deeper griefs,
whilst with my mounting troubles it keeps pace.
I cannot stop this horse of mine, nor guide it on
　　its way,
for I must go where it will go: where it stays, I
　　must stay.

Pit Pony

A red waterfall plunges over his face,
replaces a blind eye, is unable to erase the loss of ears,
the blasted half and chunks left to moulder in the mine.
Old patience, he waits for time to creak, fulfil his need,
Epona to honour an equine deal. She sometimes does.
Months tumble, slick as seconds; silence takes care of the
 rest.

Heart healed anew and sun round, halcyon Robbie
rolls whenever, runs wherever, plays long pony
days with the kid, able only to live in the now.

Epona is the goddess of horses.

Rough Horses

They are the rough horses of the common people,
grazing common land, chained by the tether of a leather
belt, moving in circles for harvesting as crops.
Should some yob or do-gooder loose the leather,
they do not pander to freedom, but meander shambolically
to feed their belly and its weight of gold.
The red bus spills riots of schoolchildren for the estate,
harsh grey uniforms on greyer pavements;
the horses prise a ponytail from the mass;
she canters towards them as feline companions slope to
    safety.
Squeezing precious carrots from a grimy pocket,
she makes the offering: Epona accepts;
the felt and whiskery lips of the goddess
nuzzle her heart until she is sated;
a yellow sun cracks open over the common.
This, then, their lot: to breathe, breed, bestow riches
in abundance and, at their end,
return to the estate, to feed their friends.

Songs of Making

Go stretch your leathery pennons,
you daymares, grown in an alien egg
to glide over numbered minutes,
your wild so wild it predates perception;
crunch withering days in razored teeth.

Go gallop on sepia stone,
you horses, lassoed by idolatry,
earth's ochre and a shaman's blood,
shadow blended. Leap the drab centuries,
awaken dull sense to colour!

Go pad across history's fields,
you felines of kohl-eyed antiquity,
couch in your dark and fathomless
judgements; betray nothing, glassy sinkholes,
complicit with the changing moon.

Take care, you children of Perses,
Gaia falters in your blundering hands:
do not unmake or be undone:
look sharp, yours is the age of the mayfly;
in a star's history, you are dead.

Animal Eden 1920

Ethereal arches answer moonlit clopping:
the long, white nose taps black fresh monument,
jerks towers of crackling bones atop his spine to mocking
    life;
they drop back to appointed places,
refuse the right to crumble; wait, as ever,
senses voided, critically teetering, infinitely holding,
enfranchised by timeless, worthless silence; wait, as ever.
The warrior's grave unlocks!
Sucked up, white confetti whirling in Utopia's wind,
all swoop into The Garden, trailing incandescent belief.

Descendants

Mount of mighty Thor, eight legged Sleipnir's
descendants wind the wild track down to matt black
    sands,
innately forming and re-forming, multicoloured horses
fly to the green and rock lands floor of Iceland,
threading themselves into the ground before ash
    spewing glaciers.

The land bears Sleipnir's print in canyoned Asbyrgi,
where he touched down, God ridden;
his heirs bidden to skate, smooth as silk, in tölt,
over dusky dunes and Arctic rocks, soothing
    spiky grasses,
bearing any for a fee, or free as friends.
One such returns as the tide, yearning for reasons.
Memories mass, blow away present like sifted snow,
stirring shades only the elves remember.

All her years of horses distil into the photograph she
    framed;
the clappety-clap speed of Gittla, sure as Sleipnir,
tölting toward, never faulting, under her descendant
    smile.

The First Cat is Reflected

By a curtained pool, where flies are apathetic,
and shadows wilt in jungle heavy lethargy,
you bend your silken head of power,
pelt flecked with hot, red victory,
survey the incomparable, and lap up perfection,
pace a flawless, rhythmic round,
molten grace and guileless glory;
spared the crippling pit of the self-aware.

Cat Couture:
Instructions for Wearing

The Macavity
luscious apparel worn loosely warm around the neck
   in winter:
if abruptly wriggly, enriches collarbone and breast
for fleetest, floor bound seconds
<u>WARNING!</u>
naked skin may protest the loss,
raising bumps of self-pity
re-wear after one/two hours

re-adorn when forlorn at any time
but do not allow tears to touch *The Macavity* –
imperative this garment does not get wet
beware sweatiness in summer

The Christie
a cravat, readily worn all day
this cat is never willingly removed, or may make
   holes
the Angel Falls negative spills from nose to navel in
   heavenly rolls
(non-optional: will deftly wash and scrub protrusions)
roundly doubles as muffler, arriving oil spill-esqe

    when seated
sumptuously stretches to wrap around the thighs
etching the heart with instantaneous reverberations

The Miggy
of nightwear, our Black Jaguar deluxe
apply to the head, ready loaded with Lethe's oblivion
winnows soporific sanity from your frenetic chaff
the nose/chin push disappears into your nape
hand shaping or caressing is involuntary –
you will acquiesce to the engine's demands
senses dim, as sleep ripples over
when last consciousness brims,
you must murmur, Je t'adore.

Conversations with my Cats: 1
Victory at Axminster

Why do you grin, tumble-turned, at the world?
Pah! The world wails it's she who's upside down,
pinned, a paper moth or milk sloppy mouse,
whining to be right side up; mine to roll
about on, rub my face in, as I please.
I rocket higher than the blood-daubed kite,
(a show-off – lets trail her fan for effect),
permit the world to winkle herself round,
then plunge, claws drawn, for the kill on her head,
V A! The ratty rug is dead! Next? Dash!

Conversations with my Cats: 2
Long Gone Beloveds

I glimpse the ghosts of *cara mia* cats.
They are here, side-seen and rippling bright
across the moss and lime green rockery,
rudders aloft, sailors on silent seas,
"Is it my love that lures you to this place?"
"No, only sun, the sun, so surely missed
by happy, holy cats: we will bathe now."
They sunshine merge with supine incumbents,
in seconds melt to limp and glossy rags,
as molten heat the buzzing garden floods.

Goodnight My Darling Girl

The sagging sun lets fall his weary rays,
a jaded age from cheeping, chirping life,
its beaks half-gagged, which once had been ablaze
with greetings and with conversations rife.
The daystar leaks his life and dying words,
written in blood across the failing sky,
"I shall return!" is slashed in sweeping swords,
"Perform your duty, fool," is my reply.
My cat selected, crept to curl her paws
around this heart, desperate for her need,
and every need was overfilled, because
an oath was sworn – cradle to grave agreed.
Death spiked her precious life; angels must weep
until poisoners find no rest in sleep.

Dorcas from Time to Time

Darkness blooms that yesterday was a bud:

we groped for one slipped away,
teetering on the vertigo of grief.

She eluded desperation, fading, chose silence,

a black and white commonplace
in matted undergrowth.

I lose, catch her flavour in another's fur,
my flow interrupted by tongue of not her;

all slivers of negatives lead to Dorcas.

In uneasy forecasts of tangled futures,
I glimpse her flickering spirit's advance,
yearn to trail a trackless courage.

Three Minutes of Butterfly Now

I lived for three whole minutes today
with every second I spent with you,
September sunshine glow on our backs,
forgetting birdsong, wind chimes, tyre tracks,
and the breeze that played with the view.

You didn't leave, though I thought you would,
through every second I spent with you,
buddleia sang the old garden's song,
Russian vine wailed the breeze was too strong;
my heartbeats lined up in a queue.

We shared a feast that September day,
those delicate seconds I spent with you,
you with your nectar, I with my eyes,
time willingly stopped – we were allies;
no beauty lived other than you.

Kestrel

The target cannot comprehend the sky,
her pitter-patter heart's horizon's bound
by grassy homelands, pinpoint nerves stand by
to shoot her undercover, safe and sound:
the kestrel's rippling fan of need digests
the current's mindless tracks; brown and curving
death is hunting, guides air to himself, crests,
holds steady, and for him, wind is swerving.
Instruction-loaded gold eyes hunt the world:
she shuffles, locks the pinpoint on her life,
from unknown skies a thunderbolt is hurled,
this ruined scrap dreamed of no afterlife.
And we, who rarely see the kill played out,
might see, might pause, might contemplate blackout.

Sharks

Mesmeric weaver, selected reliever of life;
accomplished anthem to purpose;
molten steel, sight, smell unparalleled,
the aeons honed apex of predators.
A fin of fortune, supremacy slicing the waters,
is the purchase price of death.
Caught lashing in wealth's impervious net,
the master is a flaccid jaw, finless horror, spiralling down
in ignominy; mined to the minuscule.
Dumbly, we blast balance apart,
and will deserve creation's righting.

The Flatey Experience

An island in an island, remote as a metal eye;
soft-skinned strangers alight to a concrete slab,
dumped into Freyr's truculent mist,
baiting their flaunted resolve on the ferry.

Shocked bunches of puffins bulge from a man's
 wrists;
orange beaks proclaim identity, bemoan
flight is no bulwark against death's roving eye.

The girl climbs punishing mop top mounds, one step
 up,
one step down; muscles knuckle in as relentlessly
 careless rain
floods her walking boots, attempts to drown the
 oblivious land.

Unremitting, merciless mounts grind out hot sweat, to
 the island's end.
Freyr relents, augments Iceland's holy air;
 the tombstone grin,
sunlit, awaits his unsuspecting vessel.

Hummocks melt to grainy sand; invigorated hands

freeze:
her gasp exults the God's tumescence!

His colossal, rampant, phallus-wielding effigy cows
    the sky,
humbles the mighty Atlantic! His fresh convert
    laughs, filled,
fulfilled and sown – a missionary primed to sing
    like the sea.

Flatey is pronounced flatay. Freyr is a Norse God of fair weather and fertility. Iceland's puffin population is in freefall and they are still hunted.

The Lurcher

Sliver of dappled light, sprite knifing long
grasses; white tipped, gold striped,
faster than words, rabbits

and hares, than careless birds, than thought.
Genie surfs on precipitous rocks; see a far
distant speck, blink, she's mockingly at hand;

joyous heart thrown up ahead, she trampolines
through bracken, bubblier than Champagne,
the air itself smarting at thoughtless disdain;

lithest lurcher, there in a flash and gone,
a streak in the field, competitors floundering,
bettors groan, green at how clean heels can be.

Her smart heart flips and swells,
anchors itself richlier to hands delivering
a multitude of slippery puppies.

Serenely weaving crowds and cars,
gleaning the world's welcome, mutely avowing hers,
seeds sown; she requires only to run, alone.

Time gone, carriage low, spirit straight,
glassing eyes beget blind patience, and wait.

This wise mind, deeper than mete for a dog,
sated by the world, declares it done,
is numbly borne to the oldest sleep.

Part Four
Across Time

Sorrow

She locks me out, leaning over blankets,
wipes acrid spittle from the abandoned mouth,
his body alone conducts the theatrical rattle
and is only hanging about in the wings;
she revisits, a pure and mindless moth, distilled
purpose, because it's her last act.
Time deleted hearts will open,
I am poised, leaden, for my cue.

Across Time and Space

I know the gift I'd give to you:
this leather box, velvet lined
in cobalt blue, the sea-struck blue
of your wife's eyes. Deep lines break
and falter: fear trails after stuttering synapses.

If I, untrained in death, could
pluck your gaze out from the hosts,
you'd behold oath welded gold,
guide she who drifts away.

Pre-mourning

Your world curls up,
licks the precarious past,
eyes slammed, locked
shut, to prevent the assault
of the dark.

The Singing Sea

Nanna, Nanna, never old, never known,
the sturdy love that vaults a generation,
easy as a step, grabbed stony life,
washed it behind its ears, scrubbed
and polished spit to death: hung grandad's
approbation on her private wall, content.

Idly rifling faded music, I glimpse tar ruined
essence of mezzo, melted to atoms and
atoms to the infinity of wherever and yet,

in the sleep which is not yet sleep she comes,
orchestral in the blue light, her smile of mapled
cellos widened to loose the condor, but

at a plaintive, urgent, triangle, "Nanna!"
in spectacles and Friday toys,
my Nanna rushes over me like the sea.

Do Not Ignore Now's Moment, Come What May

Do not ignore now's moment, come what may,
silenced glassy eyes in mangled cars know
galloping fate can take us as we play.

Bolshie gulls swagger, own the soaring bay,
fight scrap for scrap, tough orange eyes aglow,
do not ignore now's moment, come what may.

MS-ers and CPs two pins away
from you able-bodied folks, grin loud, show
galloping fate can't blunt us as we play.

Wild beasts know life near its wild end, delay
until a quiet deafens sound. Alone,
pursue now's lonely moment, come what may.

The blind world in its handcart strives to say,
crap deals gotta look better from below,
galloping fate, come whack us all to clay.

Oh, mummy, softly smudge the hours, or stay,
we'll give bright childhood's dice her final throw,
clasp now's burning memories, come what may,
galloping fate can fuck off for today.

Layers

A little layer peeled off today, unbidden:
slid past your sight; not like you thought;
just one of those see-through jobs
that clings to your fingers;

or maybe a fallen petal,
a neural boat broken from
its moorings and purpose.

no smell, no warning,
a shared thing isn't;
it sticks, leaden,
sacrosanct.

Icelandic Lady

Her call somersaults across the Arctic,
fizzy and dizzy and giggly with joy;
she's been flying with fulmars,
gliding in heaven,
eagerly skimming the black salty cliffs.

Friendly painted puffins pose for photos;
angry black-headed gulls shriek at the wind,
sky – ours – is – we – keep – ever!
Sod off! You – Piss off!
The lady laughs at their indignation;
at 80 she knows better than to fight.

Horses of many colours tölt the land;
she flies on golden Gittla,
churning the black sand,
Valhalla of white Siberian logs,
Sea-bleached, termite-riddled Icelandic art.

The unseen elven houses shelter the
solid art of steel and stone
her heart devours.
In endless light through nightless day, she sleeps.

Gently murmuring horizons rouse her,
filtering limpidly billowing dreams,
vast and undeniable;
she complies, quenches,
and bears witness to the skies' perfection.

The lady swims cerulean waters,
naked, energised, encircled by snow;
in this interior she
slides into herself,
does not fear Viti, crater into hell.

She rides by ropes of lava, undismayed,
sunbathes with icebergs, yearning for the sea,
walks behind God's waterfalls,
footsure and alone.
She'll stride into His bleakest winter, lone,
but not yet; she'll not anticipate.

Ancestors

They swell in summoned depths, bidden inhabit new
neurons, unable to deny the pitiful tolling of hearts;
forgotten witnesses, witnessing uselessly, mostly.

Nightly, mother's pearls are surfing, riding upon
her waves, luminous gravid moons of skin light,
slick with the passion of abiding love.

I Carry Her With Me

Windows are sea-flecked, ghost-strewn,
a tattered sky mourns,
the white lake mutters in her sleep
and you will not be stilled, you voices of disquiet,
writhing mists of dislocation.

Drowsy, I enfold her fading form, hold to hold,
breast to breast, beat to beat, mute to mute.
She cannot be with me tonight,
must fight her battle, weaponless and naked;
will forget the how of winning, the why of war.

Fossil Speak

By the light of an iron horseshoe lamp,
Orthoceras rise from their weighty tomb,
in silent, silvered relief, 396 million years
of messages from the dead, on which
your crane fly mind alights to
slide off with an archaeologist's grief
at the fossils' refusal to share.

You make a beeline for the phone to chat
with your mum, who started your history,
locked it in, and is busy deconstructing hers.

The Silver Door

She hovers in a path of intoxicating light
from the cupboard of the past, its ripened door
ajar; always she's closed it, having sipped her fill,

until this butterfly morning; at dawn she flutters
gossamer synapses, scents her father's nectar:
alights by the sleek, honeyed rivers of childhood.

She will fling the door wide open, zigzag through,
catch herself in her mother's singing net.
Who knows when she will release herself, or if.

The Necessity of Play

Cold mist twist kissed stunk miss drunk piss
The man at the top of the garden tends the fire,
not a big man, not a big fire, both fierce, hungry,
doing what they do best; hours they play,
fuelling each other, not trying to understand
uncloud, unravel, unpick, unpack, uncatch, unmask,
unbalance, unblame, unsay, unadulterate. Just play.

Modern-Day Miracles

Surgeons slide like minnows through muscle,
seductively weaving, parting capillaries, tender
and precise, to reveal the hallowed sackful
of baby swiftly shelled: another pea
of humanity, ripe for life's consumption.
Your mother, on the other hand, born in darker ages,
clutched a single ticket for a crude 10 o'clock showing,
and was gutted to find a deep furrow of lightning on her
    receipt.

A Story of Air

The old woman wavers upward,
years falling down her face,
clicks into clenched and waiting offspring,

utters the verdict carried
in the pulses of her heart – 'NO MORE
THAN LOST FEATHERS OF AGE'.

Exhalations of twisted tension
birth verdant tendrils,
arching star-wards, blessed;

trees stretch taller, further,
colours deep-mine new treasures,

creation slops over,
brands love into the thirsty body molecular.

The Road

Your road, grey, pockmarked with tarmac;
labouring upward, wheel upon wheel,
stubby legs pumping toward the village,
houses, plump with affluence, replaced
by comfortable, no, well-off homes
on your left: a gravel drive,
each stone probably hand placed,
leads to a smart, cream house
which is not yours, but does hold a whiskey-faced
    man,
like your dad's, you see too much of him Friday
    nights;
next up is the Dalmatian's,
ball bouncy, spotty and fat,
he'll die soon you think, he's called Roger
but his people are strange,

and strangely Roger doesn't die.
A grass verge has followed you all the way,
like a puppy, peeing saplings
for village yobs to vandalise,
often succeeding:
years later, they'll stop replanting.
Never mind, two have made it,
more than two of the yobs.
On your right, it's called the Bank:
heathland grasses running free,
carelessly spreading their seed,
sprint all the way down past the quarry,
and the council estate,
where foal-a-year rough horses
graze to the mud, leather belts around their necks.
Now, finally, you see the massive trees.
They are the only two for miles; evergreen, muscular
branches draped in viciously-long pine needles,
not for climbing, try it and you die.

One sprouted a Union Jack in '77
aided by dared, pickled hands at 4am;
you awoke, shrieked in shock
and pride as he snored.
low castle walls each side growl –
useless for protecting a house whose back door's
 always open.
And now you make the turn, peach tree in sight,
protected by gruff Yorkshire stone with its glass
 house
bulging out like a pregnancy,
so you wheel in on your trike, your bike with
 stabilisers,
your bike, your bike, bearing oaty and sugar beet
bucketfuls of pony nuts,
your minivan borrowed from work, your Ford Fiesta,
loaned by dad,
your Ford Fiesta, left by dad, your own Polly Polo,
your stick, your sticks, your walker, your wheeled

mobility aid,

and introducing the last act, Tonto the Pronto, your trusty wheelchair.

No more trees, no more drive, no more peaches, no more house,

no more road.

No more you.

The Oak

Sapling slender,

she stands in the ruins,

bearing a beacon of safety

for the kids, shot down by cruelty,

splattered with selfishness,

strung out, bewildered.

Her roots are wider, deeper,

stronger than he can conceive:

She is The Oak.

Rage

You did not go gently nor peacefully,
my friend, so smart, so seething.
You told wise doctors you knew
your evicted for sure cancer
had slunk home. What was their answer?
"It's usual, for sure, it's in your head."
Twice dread words stayed unsaid.
Finally, it's confirmed they said, for sure,
but "sorry, after all, you're eighty-four."
Chaff is cherished, pomposity regarded,
Young fools encouraged, wisdom discarded.
Oh, Mr Thomas, would you'd lived 'til age,
and found going gently's preferable to rage.

Green Lane

The market's quilted cobblestones feast the eyes,
bounce your bottom like a tennis ball as you make
for Mr Magic who can fix your broken purse.

Inaccessible pubs overflow cosy with gnarled, nicotine
leaky beams: dad would sniff his bloodhound's way
to every bar, polish it over riotous years with patched

elbow and bonhomie, drunks hoisting his skinny frame
in the chair, shoulder high over steps, if he were you,
and not dead. You plunder imagination from desire.

Green Lane nibbles the Chevin's heel, tipsy with
cowslips and feathery ferns. *All right, Bunny?*
he asks, loping the never was, never looking back.

The Need for Protection

Protection tracks our lucky baby heels, toddler flop,
collapsed cartwheel, juvenile implosion, sodden slip in
    muddy years,
flying lunge to greener ground. Else bitter life could
pounce, and shake us till we're dead.

Your mum is the egg, the jewel you stash in the
    ultimate safe,
float in cotton wool, swaddle; no pressure,
or the shell cracks, the diamond fractures, and tears of
    mislaying
undo both your faces.

Your dad was fourteen days dead, when he zapped
    you in the car
on the M1, heading south, "Goodbye Bunny." No
    more, as per,
no disintegrating mountain wept, no star fell, no
    wailing remnant loitered,
"Bye dad." Floored, elated.

If your luck flows true, it might halloo you home to
    stoic heath,
and silver birch, cleaved by glossy water, under a

    Yorkshire bridge.
Here, the thing you named your soul might thank you,
before turning out the light.

You startle yourself with need, bewildered by sinking
    opportunities,
treacherous age shrinks your galleons to coracles; you
    snap lifeboat
heels three times, for nothing: paper luck disintegrates.

Astonished souls flare joy and recognition. You know
    the stranger, never seen,
jump into the new, now two and evermore shall be
    so; hug yourselves to Otley.

Good Hearts

I met you on the day he died, husband of forty years,
his heart so full of love it burst. You dropped to your
workaday knees to salvage chips of him
to polish, pocket and protect.

Dream now, fly, catch his wild heart, fling your arms
    about it,
clutch the black jacket,
hair streaming, screaming life; out-race Pendle's
witches as a feral wind lashes the fell.

Three Days of Christmas

1991

His distilled time and humour:
meekly sliding mud down the pillows,
"Do you want to move up?"
"Why, do you want to get in?"
Heaped mourners are gifted
priceless, desperate laughter.

The sheets are blank, defensive,
claiming his bones; they knew,
not we; this day, his last but two;
(they came to wrenched nothings,
he'd scarpered to soak up nacreous
sunshine in morphined Ibiza.)

2011

My four-wheeled electric fortress murmurs,
scrabbles on the fringes of knowing,
"I'm on drugs too now, Dad, can I get in?"
Cool air trickles sand, the universe chimes,
songs of pitted moons echo the source,
the curtain parts a millisecond; closes.

The Case

It sits in the attic, at the top of faded stairs, past
the broken spinning wheel, a lonely string
unravelling forever, or until someone pulls it out,
and the rusty trunk of always useful, never used blankets.

The muscular catches snap satisfyingly open, the lid
    whoofs up,
releasing its soap-smelly treasure. He is there, waiting,
grinning, filling the Giggleswick School blazer, navy
with a thin, red stripe, although I might be wrong;
maybe it was wrapped in a fog of plastic, to hang
on the rail with frock coats, furs and Nanna's 50s
    glories,
tutting at mum's forsaken glamour; theatrical
    accumulations.

The double act of grin and blazer swing around the
    door,
as we liberate our bopping hearts through Come on
    Eileen
and Enola Gay, but we dump The Ant's sexy thigh
    boots,
for the Giggleswick Lad is reborn, joyously assuming

he surprises,
boozily confident of hearty welcomes on fourteen
    pints and whiskey chasers,
trenches of silent griefs and disappointments eradicated.

He sways in to catch his wife. They waltz, dropped
out of time, any time; the room staggers giggles and
    guffaws,
shamelessly, giddily whirling: we are sparklers waving
    at heaven.

The stranger in black is prowling, circling, closing in on
    him
as the beat goes on. For pity's sake, close the lid.

Part Five
Green Daze

The Glen Woods

Under these faded skies, all paths lead into the woods,
their lodestone: sandy, rocky, lined with ponies
or nettles, or scuttering down to the triangular dam,
    filmy with dragonflies,
or muddily weaving alongside the beck, wiggling its
    toes in the waters,
past the cup-and-ring, a crude, Neolithic design,
    whose secrets are
hidden by laughing green abundance, nestling close to
    its silent partner,
a blink-and-you-miss-it spring, pooling under
    celandines and ladybirds.

There was an autumn walk up hawthorned Birdcage,
    heavy with wild garlic,
mired by summer-fat horses' shoes, mud hugging my
    walking boots,
past the kissing gate which I never got to use, but
    stop! Stop right there –
hung on a spider's thread are clumsy teenage lips
    upon mine;
I cast about for his face, was there a nearly leather
    jacket or grey fleece …
I clutch – the thread is blown away and we are gone.

The oaks wait stoically for the next ice age, but I have
 had mine,
and cushion into the comfort of a familiar hand on
 my thigh.
I am sucked in with the tracks, seeking the nectar of
 the oak, ash,
silver birch and sycamores, clutching their helicopter
 babies:
but the oaks are torpedoed by brown leaf sickness,
 and yet mourn the elms
whose ghosts shimmer sadly, cured of lingering death.

Green Daze

The whirlpooled Strid is hidden to me now,
but slow trundled paths are mine; my chair
rocks, bucking side to side, fruitlessly trying
to rid itself of me like a new-backed colt.
I rumble, thunder to a world, light unveiled;
all dreamers and poets must surely be here.
The trees, Oh God! the trees! Gaia's gauntlet
to death; grandfathers replace my baby breath;
living giants, born exalted to splatter the sky;
dark spring and India greens, seared by apple
lightning, branch to toe; lime and forest
mops of unruly offspring surge to freedom,
candle flicker the limitless, waving, giggling,
dapple me green, dare me to cannonball,
feral and sap-full, shedding snug limits.
And should giants speak, I would comply,
to stand, unsteady as a breeze-mocked sapling,
there plant my roots, merge me with my Earth.

Garden Grass

Grass is grafted in from the heathland,
deliberately drafted in whole by her ignorant hands,
divining dark need in the childhood gorge of her gut;
soil thrust, it thrives amongst the delicate, the
    off-come-d'uns,
her celestial city, dew pretty, bejewelled ones.
But old worms are bold amongst the buds,
beyond biblical epochs arrive as seeds drift down,
ancient roots snake along youthful conduits,
construct webs, conduct insidious, lengthy invasions;
    multiply.
Leisurely tsunamis, they suffocate the innocents,
    pardoning none;
making examples of those so lately come, so greatly
    prized, so young.
Heathland marks time, ceaselessly serene,
unhurriedly enveloping all tracks and traces of
    interlopers;
masses on high ground, undated,
and in a baited breath, we are gone.

One Chevin December

The gravid sky lumbers in overnight,
fog's up, morose and threatening;
swaddled, you trace, retrace steps
through spiky trees, calling the dog;
she flashes past, a scrap of beating
thunder, fast receding, blotted out.
Splattered remnants of last week's
snow on the evergreens' arms,
reach out to freeze the moisture
on your face; but you are snorting
anger's fire, to staunch the pitiful salt,
and turn your back on piebald beauty.

Shell Dreaming

Wan hands clamber around netted,
lifeless, watercolour shells;
faded laver spires, kitten's paws,

dog whelks, angel's wings,
bone whites; a white so white
you follow, like Alice, down
the dark hole of the head.

A sun, a sea, a four-year-old world;
crayon-blue, coral-frilled, stubby legs
pumping a burgeoning will;

squatted on unpoppable seaweed
of tinkle yellow and brownie browns,
thick slippery and mountain ranged;

starfish fingers out-splay on inky rocks
by mussel skies and periwinkles;
eyes new drink a sea-soaked Eden;

flitter fishes, hearty barnacles, mobile bedsits,
(crabs of indefinite intentions),
colour dance through sun flashed ripples;

Dawdling days of puppy fat plenty,
mimicked yesterday and tomorrow,
yawning stretch that drowsy summer.

Relentless months tug at her teeth,
the universe waits in the pool;
sea grass grows long in her hair,
necklace shells sing down her breast.

There's only the now, and now is gone,
kicking hard for the horizon,
discarding abandoned homes and years
for a deep and painful blue.

Winter Prison

Winter Prison 1

Your prison is too soon draped in November,
wrapped in boneless leaves, they cling to your wheels,
and you bring them inside, as if time spent
with warmth invading their cells
will bring them back to life.

Winter Prison 2

If the neat mortician unwraps your heart
like a Seville orange, he'll be knocked out
to reveal at its core
the vermilion flames of your sumac,
which have kept you frost-free.

Winter Prison 3

How do you know when it's all over
for you in your suffocating cell?
a last breath? a gurgle?
A slight, white bugger shoots you in the head,
bellows, REGENERATION!

Bad Spring

She poos noddy snowdrops, prises apart crocus eyelids,
eyeballs crows, demolishes despised daddy's glittering
 legacy,
flings down stars-of-Jerusalem; stony earth's attitude
 softens;
she barges out, rupturing soil with polyanthus acne;
spies compelling knobs, tugs, jerks, shrieks jostles of
 bottomless beaks,
raw curls of rodents, globs of gloopy spawn;
 splatters primary colours
the garden had all but forgot in its interminable
 incarceration.
Amplifying, she deafens dawn with happening
 orchestras,
looses monstrous, verdant tsunamis, gobs rain,
 vanishes.
Marched back by time, pissed off and resentful, flies
 black and white
infanticide in sulky pique, challenges Luna's zealots to
 worship 24/7;
claws are sharpened, piteous sacrifices made.
She hurls herself upon maturity, yanks a hapless sun
 to his zenith,

ruthlessly sucks on his nuclear core, climaxes and,
as the clematis births with a sigh of perfection,
grudgingly embraces her daughter's soporific balm.

'77 Hot Summer Drops

Lungfuls of old creosote from the dog-chewed bench
launch staccato memories –
manefuls of new-mown hay fold obediently,
juvenile muscles aching from the scythe,
having worked a meagre of the acre;
yappy barks invade a close-cropped field,
heckling cavaletti-hopping ponies;
silky cats, leopard-style in purring branches,
or brazenly flopped on patio stones, flash frying at
    full stretch,
ignoring emancipated trills within swiping distance:
every drop of luscious sun sucked out of summer.

The Crying Leaves

Leaves moan and weep under deliberate feet,
crashing on each crackling cursing other, wail
remember vaulting green and gay and bulging
veins blood-bloated and sky-smooth skin high
billowing over Earth in parental dominion.

Age gnashes as grainy heels and wheels hard grind
sending slack, obstinate bodies to cold coffins, or age
mulched in dog piss and undulating whimpers or
frostbitten skeletons and tenuous ghosts confused
confused and begging for the dream-distant past.

September View

Half cut from the pub and 15 days away
from the garden, you return to find fifty
bees in amour with lavender sedum.
Buzz-slapped and reeling, you watch work,
after the bitterest night, drink in the gold,
regardless. Your heady gaze floats upward,
gasps at a treasure, awaited all negligent
summer; the casual butterfly drinks deep
in amber solitude; you do not know you breathe.

Goit Stock

They do not stop because you are not there,
Goit Stock's bright waters fall now as they did,
giggling, sparkling, caught in the glare
of spring's young sun, dappling twigs, amid
bracken and gay fern; pooling and creeping
up thighs of half-naked, gravestone-grey rocks,
fountaining feathers, pronking and sweeping
icicle days into spring equinox.
Your will denies your homing instinct tug,
renounces Eden for a concrete bed,
plays diva and tramp, weighed down by your shrug,
wading thick time, forgetting why you fled.
Goit Stock admits no change; its afterglow
will find you; let the healing waters flow.

Part Six
Epiphany

Leaving

She didn't mean to leave
when she left; glasses
and paper accusatory,

abandoned on the cusp
of purpose; a sonnet,
a Jane Eyre, perhaps.

No scratched marks of life:
a refined, elegant fade,
often thought best. Truth,

a splayed mess, ought
never to be seen in public:
but death's uncouth.

From the Other Side

You chose to go, and I wonder
if your implacable decision forming
fundamentals were imperfect,
when you tiptoed, whirled, strode
or thundered to your assignation
with your under-polished oven
and its ruthless breath.
Does your vibrant spirit sometimes
wander to the great wall to watch
us doing dishes, splashing ephemeral
bubbles born to die, gorging ourselves
on sensation, and do you feel desire?

Old Man Gone

His head is sticky with shredded thoughts,
wheeled through blinding crowds by unseen hands,
their high-pitched babble useless as static.
He has no sextant, compass or maps of now,
until the buzz of all buzzes rattles the skinny frame:
nostrils jumpstart, scenting their rheumy way skyward;
history's tears are wind-snatched as the past bellows
his name and rank, severing dusty decades. He rises,
an eagle, to soar with the Spitfire in the sun.

Faces

You do not blur, faces of kindness, tracing the places
  an angel sips his fill.
Strangers offer unforeseen amity as raindrops animate
  the desert;
until my chair had finally found me, my legs' wild
  wandering chained,
I never knew the glory and abundance of the rain.

They saw tears in a foreign land,
drew near, spent time to touch a hand, weave away an
  evening;
speech blind, none could clutch or woo words to
  understanding,
so I signed my gratitude, and entwined my heart with
  each.

A Mohican, grim, strides over the bridge, leather
  jacket flying,
tattooed head, blatant packet on display – an
underhanded knife behind his back?
changes tack to my side, slows; I, stranded, freeze,
  second-guessing,
drops to his knees, secures my distressingly undone
  shoe;

like I said, I never knew.

Need unleashes kindness, roaming rain falls on the
   dune,
now pitter-patter ever faster torrents teeming down
   from heaven,
in every alleyway and street, drum shattering
   crescendos deafen:
I thank all glorious gods, for the endless monsoon's
   lesson.

Laments

One

Has the winter stopped singing and can we play
new tunes of wonder, promise and regret?
Who did not know somebody lost in the howling
that lashed across the land (a parent, a friend,
the long-lost friend of a friend, a bird). The turning of
so-called seasons, blurring, doesn't change rules.
Years lie dead. Millions of souls flown,
flapping sorrowful goodbyes, are lost to the stars.
He is gone; I supped on pain. Today I bury my head
in the spring, sipping green waters, tasting the now.

Two

Are you awake, Greymalkin, the wicked wind awaits
    you,
your lady moon pulses blood orange: taste her on your
pink tongue, touch her with your wide whiskers, catch
    her,
roll her in green concentration, smother her under your
    chin.
I am awake, daemon; I relish my bloody orb's fatal
    power

on cold graveyards, old black incantations; her portents
 ripen;
candles flutter in the twisted air; claws scutter, await
 execution:
I yearn, yowl, but the mewling door is shut! I cannot
 play tonight!

The Mirror

The willow weeps lime green and yellow lays, to
    lullaby the river into sleep,
somnolent summer airs faintly brush across his
    breadth,
dappling and dimming him to placid, glassy depths,
bearing helpless witness to arching flawlessness;
midges mill and skeeters skate;

a maned head glides through, forcing form to
    whirling cloud;
sucked under, slain by the lustful river's longest kiss;
a body palely trails behind, surrendering its treasures,
reluctant to roll over and break her last embrace,
until caught on a shattered scream.

The mother hauls herself to tired feet, to meet a
    foretold bell;
the mirror, unable to enfold her shattering, is left
    vast emptiness.

Insha Allah 2015

Horror on their backs, whipping them on,
home and family deleted at the feather
touch of a button: resolute flames of hope
illuminate their tattered lives; they huddle,
hip to hip, fate to fate, on prayer-soaked sands,
as pockmarked Syria sinks underneath them.

Squashed on a floating penny, survival flares
in panicked hearts, hope flicks off and on,
and all histories condense to Insha Allah.
The avaricious iron sea will eat their stories,
as Europe sleeps, but not all; not all, Insha Allah.

Play Day Diaries

Grumbled awake, we roll into slots,
side-by-side and two by two, snapped
by infants into four-wheeled Tonka trucks.
We are silent, sour, sweet or gobby, you,
drunk on play day mirth or leaking incredulity.

Decanted into plastic chairs in bald community
rooms, we slam down desperate dominoes, stick or
twist the morning, win thin old pennies, lose interest.

Come lunchtime, we feed on luscious raspberry
    gossip:
a silver tramp's winkled her wrinkles into studded
    black
leather, stroked the shrivelled willy of a billionaire,
to end up, end up, trussed up and sent up on a private
    747!
Fall out of damp chairs in green laughter.

Slide the wilted slope of afternoon; 4:15
prompt bundle up, roll out; day done; wait,
collected gobblers of nothing others want,
enjoying nowhere anybody wants to go.

On a Southport Sunday

Trios of pink-footed geese
fly purposefully past sun
startled windows.

The lake simpers,
tickling five-star swans,
and brisk white triangles.

Sandals are fearless
thongs down Lord Street;
blatant adolescents

who have no word for
autumn; they weave,
bottomless, transparent,

reek of burgeoning,
jump on the wind's wheel,
cleave to nascent pride.

Earnest dogs pummel
pavements; park, grinning,
in cafés, end-of-line bins,
no muffin-necks or fat ducks;

tail-waggers wait at table,
collecting strangers in quick licks.
Miniature Munroes and Bacalls
strut or are cradled, satisfied
eyes oozing self-worth.

This is wheel town, where
hills are discouraged and
the sea too lazy to kiss the pier;

a Penny Farthing and the 'other
one' parade importantly down
its length, dutifully impressive.

The afternoon rolls over to doze
and dream of African sands; a lone
moped bustles about, without note.

The lake flings fake blue undies
at a disdainful sky; unrifled,
she flounces in ruffles and pouts.

Painted horses leap for kiddiwinks
but 6 o'clock has scarpered
to the next eastern seaboard.

The beachball sun deflates with rosy sighs;
slack formation geese arrow

sleepwards, honks muted and replete.

The evening spits high heels, willing
tonight to be at first sight; barely legal
young stags drink and own the world.

Dusky billows long for the bosky island,
a fading sky hints weakly of his past;
the swan-empty, unchallenged lake relaxes

into molten metal, white as Pegasus;
the old Irish Sea comes regularly,
foaming at heckling from the moon;

sucked out of midnight, Monday
rubs her eyes as constellations
race to beat Apollo's nags.

Dvořák in Bradford

The mermaid wakes the cello,
wraps her sea-silk tail around its heart,
enchants a pulsing horn to echo dance
upon waves of chattering violins.
Mindful, The Hallé splashes through.

The cello groans, whale-deep,
surfaces to glide on fulmar's wings,
dives hungrily down to splinter,
into shoals of fluttering quavers.
Mindful, The Hallé ripples through.

Intermittently, I muse, distracted,
on sharp pains of complicated life,
dragged back by the mermaid's swell,
re-lost to time in the dark hole of me.
Mindful, The Hallé deepens through.

The mermaid flies the albatross to streaks of lone
intensity: the gathered storm's unleashed! Ripping
    through,
crashing all around, before and inside. Dies instantly.
Time stops in frozen obeisance.
Realised, The Hallé thunders through!
Accumulated worshippers flood, drown and reprise

and reprise:
leave me glory-drenched on unknown shores:
    Epiphany.

Bennison Books

Bennison Books has four imprints:

Contemporary Classics
Great writing from new authors

Non-Fiction
Interesting and useful works written by experts

People's Classics
Handpicked golden oldies by favourite and forgotten authors

Poetic Licence
Poetry and prosetry

Bennison Books is named after Ronald Bennison, an aptly named blessing.

Bennisonbooks.com

A good book is a blessing

Printed in Poland
by Amazon Fulfillment
Poland Sp. z o.o., Wrocław